For the Teacher

This reproducible study guide to use in conjunction with *Toliver's Secret* consists of lessons for guided reading. Written in chapter-by-chapter format, the guide contains a synopsis, pre-reading activities, vocabulary and comprehension exercises, as well as extension activities to be used as follow-up to the novel.

In a homogeneous classroom, whole class instruction with one title is appropriate. In a heterogeneous classroom, reading groups should be formed: each group works on a different novel at its own reading level. Depending upon the length of time devoted to reading in the classroom, each novel, with its guide and accompanying lessons, may be completed in three to six weeks.

Begin using NOVEL-TIES for reading development by distributing the novel and a folder to each child. Distribute duplicated pages of the study guide for students to place in their folders. After examining the cover and glancing through the book, students can participate in several pre-reading activities. Vocabulary questions should be considered prior to reading a chapter; all other work should be done after the chapter has been read. Comprehension questions can be answered orally or in writing. The classroom teacher should determine the amount of work to be assigned, always keeping in mind that readers must be nurtured and that the ultimate goal is encouraging students' love of reading.

The benefits of using NOVEL-TIES are numerous. Students read good literature in the original, rather than in abridged or edited form. The good reading habits, formed by practice in focusing on interpretive comprehension and literary techniques, will be transferred to the books students read independently. Passive readers become active, avid readers.

Novel-Ties® are printed on recycled paper.

SYNOPSIS

Ten-year-old Ellen Toliver and her mother live in New York with Ellen's grandfather during the time of the American Revolution. Ellen's father was killed at the Battle of Brooklyn Heights, and the family has received no word of her brother, who had gone to fight with his father. Ellen is confused when she sees her grandfather put his snuffbox inside of a bread her mother is baking. He does not explain, but warns her to say nothing of what she has seen.

While Ellen is getting water at the pump, her grandfather falls on the ice and sprains his ankle. He reveals to Ellen that he is a Patriot spy and that the snuffbox in the bread contains an important message for General Washington. Unable to deliver the bread himself, he proposes that Ellen do it disguised as a boy. She is to take a boat across New York Harbor to Elizabeth-town, New Jersey and deliver the bread to Mr. Shannon at the Jolly Fox Tavern. Ellen, who has always considered herself timid and lacking in courage, agrees to go when her grandfather impresses upon her the importance of the mission.

Things start to go wrong when the Brinkerhoff boys steal the bread from Ellen while she is heading for the docks. She retrieves the bread, but loses precious time. When she arrives at the docks, the only boats available are those carrying British troops. As Ellen engages in conversation with two British soldiers, Dow and Higgins, she is whisked aboard their boat by Dow, who covets her bread. She saves the loaf by tucking it under her jacket, doubling up, and locking her arms beneath her legs. To pacify the hungry soldier, she offers him some corncakes. Ellen then makes friends with Higgins, who gives her advice on how to overcome fear by concentrating on the task at hand.

When the boat docks, Ellen discovers that she is in Perth Amboy, not Elizabeth-town. Faced with a ten-mile walk, Ellen accepts an offer from Mr. Murdock, a farmer, to ride with him on his horse. When Ellen drops her precious loaf, she makes him stop so that she can retrieve it from a stream.

Stopping at Murdock's farm, which is half a mile from Elizabeth-town, Ellen is treated to dinner. When Mrs. Murdock insists that Ellen remove her wet breeches, she flees from the house, fearful of being discovered as a girl. In her haste, she forgets the bread and watches in horror as Mrs. Murdock throws the bread to a pig. Ellen overcomes her fear of pigs to retrieve the loaf.

With her loaf in hand, Ellen begins the walk to Elizabeth-town in the dark. She soon spies a light ahead, which is coming from a blacksmith's shop. Inside she finds the smith with a man getting his horse shod. When the men question her about what she is carrying under her jacket, the girl becomes frightened and leaves.

Ellen finally locates the tavern, but is distressed when a woman inside tells her that Mr. Shannon is out of town. The woman later identifies herself as Mrs. Shannon and leads the girl to her husband, the same man who was with the smith. At last, Ellen is able to hand the bread over to Mr. Shannon.

When Ellen returns home with news of her adventures, her mother and grandfather are shocked by all the trouble she had. The adventure has given Ellen a great deal of self-confidence. The family soon receives good news. Grandfather's snuffbox comes back to him with a message that Washington was able to take the city of Trenton. The family also learns that Ellen's brother, now a sergeant, is safe and well in Morristown. There is one more surprise for Ellen—a silver locket, which she likes to pretend came from General Washington himself.

BACKGROUND INFORMATION

The American Colonies 1763–1776

Before 1763 most colonists were loyal to England whose laws ruled the American colonies. After gaining vast territories at the end of the French and Indian War in 1763, England decided to maintain a standing army in North America. The British paid for this venture by taxing the colonists with laws such as the **Stamp Act of 1765**. Americans viewed such acts as ways of taking money from them without their consent since they were not represented in Parliament. Parliament repealed the Stamp Act in 1766, but the **Townshend Acts of 1767** levied duties on tea, lead, paint, and paper. Because of strong colonial opposition, Parliament repealed these taxes, except for the levy on tea.

Other events aroused colonial public opinion against England. Boston became a particular hotbed of discontented citizens, and England felt compelled to garrison the city. In March 1770, when a group of British soldiers were harassed by some Boston citizens, the fracas soon escalated. A gathering mob threatened the soldiers, who panicked and fired into the crowd, resulting in the deaths of five colonists. Passionate Americans blew the incident out of proportion, calling it the **Boston Massacre**.

In 1773 Parliament passed the **Tea Act**. It made British tea the cheapest on the American market, forcing out foreign competitors. To protest, Boston colonists boarded ships loaded with English tea and dumped it overboard. This event became known as the **Boston Tea Party**.

The British retaliated by passing the **Intolerable Acts of 1774**, which closed the Boston harbor, removed some powers from colonial governments, outlawed town meetings, required that those accused of some crimes be tried outside the colonies, and allowed British troops to take over taverns and live free of charge in private homes. By this time the colonies began to unite, forming a **Continental Congress** to discuss their mutual concerns and protest against British actions.

On April 19, 1775, the British opened fire on the main supply arsenal at Lexington. A band of colonial fighters, called Minutemen, defended the arsenal. When the British moved to destroy the depot at Concord, news of the death of eight Lexington Minutemen brought out many colonists willing to fight the British troops, which were forced back to Boston.

After the **battles at Lexington and Concord**, the war officially began with the **Declaration of Independence (July 4, 1776)**. Although much public opinion had built up against England by this time, only one-third of Americans were Patriots favoring independence, another third remained neutral, and the rest were Tories remaining loyal to Britain.

The novel *Toliver's Secret* begins in December 1776, when the Revolutionary War had barely begun.

The Battle of Long Island

In July 1776, British General Howe landed on Staten Island with 34,000 men to uproot General George Washington and his troops in New York City. Washington was in a dangerous situation on Manhattan Island, and he further weakened his army by sending part of his troops across to Long Island to fortify Brooklyn Heights. The British landed 20,000 troops on Long Island on August 22. The Americans were defeated in a fierce battle on August 27, after which the remains of the American army on Long Island ferried back to Manhattan.

Battle of Kips Bay

On August 30, 1776, General Howe attempted to negotiate with the Americans, hoping to find them disheartened after their defeat on Long Island. This failing, Howe decided to pursue Washington and his troops. On September 13, British warships and transports began to move up the East River. During the morning of September 15, colonial militia units along Kips Bay were bombarded from British frigates, while more than 80 flatboats laden with soldiers massed behind the warships. The American militia defenders abandoned their trenches and fled inland. General Washington, on horseback, tried in vain to hold his men to their duty. The retreat of the American forces allowed New York City to fall into British hands.

Battle of White Plains

In October 1776, realizing that he was vulnerable to British sea power as long as he remained on Manhattan Island, General Washington withdrew across King's Bridge. The evacuation was completed when, late in October, General Howe sent a fleet up the East River into Long Island Sound and landed troops in Westchester County, New York. He caught up with the Americans at White Plains. Although defeated in the all-day battle on October 28, Washington withdrew before the enemy could drive in for the kill. A few days later he crossed the Hudson into New Jersey. Howe, instead of following, returned to Manhattan Island.

Battle of Trenton

General Washington received reinforcements from the army he had left behind in New York, and the state of Pennsylvania raised some militia. On Christmas night of 1776, while the Pennsylvania militia distracted other troops to the southeast, Washington crossed the Delaware and captured about 1,000 celebrating Hessians (German soldiers-for-hire) at Trenton, New Jersey. Encouraged by his success, Washington decided to go after other enemy outposts in New Jersey. He crossed the Delaware once again, only to be cornered by General Cornwallis at Assunpink Creek east of Trenton on January 2, 1777. Cornwallis, however, postponed the attack until morning, allowing Washington and his men to escape.

Battle of Princeton

After escaping Cornwallis, Washington made his way toward Princeton, where he ran into three British regiments on January 3. The Americans won a narrow victory and managed to escape before Cornwallis could bring reinforcements up from Trenton. Washington then marched on to the hills at Morristown, where he went into winter quarters.

HISTORICAL PEOPLE IN THE NOVEL

General Charles Cornwallis

British general who was sent to America with reinforcements for General William Howe. He took part in the battle of Long Island, the capture of New York, and the occupation of Philadelphia.

King George III

King of England during the time of the American Revolution. He used his money and position to influence Parliament. The King supported George Grenville, who became prime minister in 1763. It was Grenville who initiated the unpopular Stamp Act. The King was in full agreement with all the British actions that resulted in war with the American colonies.

General William Howe

English general sent to Boston with reinforcements for General Thomas Gage, British Commander in Chief for North America. Howe played a distinguished part in the battle of Bunker Hill, succeeded Gage as commander of British troops in the colonies, and was knighted. In 1776 he landed on Long Island, defeated the American troops, and captured New York City.

Thomas Paine

American Revolutionary writer and pamphleteer. Through his strong prose, Paine helped change American minds in favor of independence. In January 1776 he issued *Common Sense*, a forty-two page pamphlet that became the most influential American book ever printed by fueling American passion against England.

George Washington

Commander in Chief of the American Army in the Revolutionary War and first President of the United States. When Washington took command of the Continental Army outside Boston on July 2, 1775, there was no staff at headquarters, no strategic plan, and no information; the army itself was neither disciplined nor experienced. It was Washington through his own strength of character who created a formidable Continental force and who helped keep it together.

PRE-READING ACTIVITIES

1. Preview the book by reading the title and the author's name and by looking at the illustration on the cover. What do you think the book will be about? When and where does it take place? Have you read any other books on the same subject?

2. Read the Background Information on pages two and three of this study guide and do some additional research to learn about the events that led up to the American Revolution and some of the early battles of the war. Using a K-W-L chart, such as the one below, record some facts that you know in the first column, ask questions in the second column, and fill in the third column after you finish the book.

American Revolution

What I Know –K–	What I Want to Find Out –W–	What I Learned –L–

3. Using your knowledge of the American Revolution, classify each item in the box below under the heading "Pro-American" or "Pro-British." Do as many as you can before reading the book. Complete the rest as you read.

General Cornwallis	King George III	Hessians
General Howe	Lobsterbacks	Thomas Paine
Patriots	Rebels	Redcoats
Tories	General Washington	Yankees

Pro-American   **Pro-British**

_____   _____

_____   _____

_____   _____

_____   _____

_____   _____

_____   _____

4. Discuss the meaning of the word "courage." What different kinds of courage are there? Can someone or something give you courage, or does it come from within? Can someone be afraid and still exhibit courage? Do you consider yourself a courageous person? Why or why not?

Pre-Reading Activities (cont.)

5. Draw a line from each military term on the left to its definition on the right. Use a dictionary if necessary.

   1. bayonet
   2. cannon
   3. militia
   4. musket
   5. regiment
   6. squad

   a. citizen soldiers
   b. daggerlike steel weapon attached to the muzzle of a gun
   c. military unit usually made up of ten to twelve persons
   d. heavy, large caliber gun used by infantry soldiers: predecessor of modern rifle
   e. unit of ground forces consisting of two or more battalions
   f. mounted gun for firing heavy projectiles

6. *Toliver's Secret*, which takes place during the American Revolution, is a work of historical fiction—one that uses history as a background for imagined events. The characters in such a work may be fictional or historical or both. Read about the Historical People in the Novel on page four of this study guide. Then do some additional research to learn more about each of these people. As you read the novel, determine whether the author has accurately portrayed these historical figures.

7. Esther Wood Brady, the author of *Toliver's Secret*, said of her writing:

   The characters in my books are imaginary, but their times and lifestyles seem very real to me.*

   In what ways do authors make their characters' times and lifestyles seem real? Do you think this is more important in pieces of historical fiction than in other works? Support your answer with examples from books that you have read.

*From *Something about the Author*, Vol. 31, p. 35. (Detroit, Gale Research, 1983)

CHAPTERS 1, 2

Vocabulary: Use the words in the Word Box and the clues below to complete the crossword puzzle.

WORD BOX
auburn
blustering
drayman
haughtily
impish
jauntily
mimic
minuet
nimbly
pendulum
rafters
roister
smirking
snuffbox
tavern
waistcoat

Across

1. weight hung from a fixed point so as to swing to and fro under the force of gravity
3. mischievous
6. man's vest
9. talking noisily and violently
10. place where alcoholic drinks are sold and drunk
14. lightly and quickly
15. smiling in a self-satisfied way
16. be lively and noisy

Down

2. make fun of by imitating
4. scornfully
5. person who drives a low, strong cart or wagon for carrying heavy loads
7. small box for holding powdered tobacco taken into the nose
8. smartly; stylishly
11. slanting beams of a roof
12. reddish brown
13. slow, stately dance with complex figures, popular in the 1600s and 1700s

Chapters 1, 2 (cont.) p. 3 - 31

Read to find out whether Grandfather is pro-American or pro-British.

Questions:

1. What makes Ellen think that her grandfather has lost his wits? What does his behavior suggest?

2. What surprising thing does Ellen's grandfather do with his snuffbox? What is his reaction when he realizes that Ellen has been watching him?

3. Why are six British soldiers living in Grandfather's house?

4. What evidence shows that Grandfather, Mother, and Ellen are not loyal to the British?

5. Why doesn't Ellen like to go to the pump? How do Ellen's mother and grandfather differ about the way Ellen should handle the situation?

6. Why are Ellen and her mother living with Grandfather?

7. What services other than haircuts and shaves might a colonial barber, such as Grandfather, perform?

8. Why does Ellen run away from Dicey?

9. What happens to Grandfather while Ellen is at the pump?

Questions for Discussion:

1. Why do you think Ellen's mother and grandfather do not want Ellen to know the reason why the snuffbox was placed inside the bread?

2. Why do you think Grandfather is so upset about his sprained ankle?

Literary Element: Setting

In literature, the setting refers to the time and place in which the story events occur. What is the setting of this novel?

_____

What details about the setting make the characters' times and lifestyles seem real?

_____

_____

_____

Chapters 1, 2 (cont.)

Literary Device: Point of View

Point of view in literature refers to the voice telling the story. When one of the characters acts as a narrator, it is called a first person point of view. When the author as an outside observer tells the story, it is called a third person point of view. From what point of view is *Toliver's Secret* told?

_____

Why do you think the author chose this point of view?

_____

_____

_____

Science Connection:

Ellen's grandfather uses leeches to treat bruises and swellings. Do some research to find out how these worms were once used to treat the sick. For what illnesses was this treatment used? How far back in history can this treatment be traced? How effective was it and why? Do some additional research to learn how leeches are used for medical purposes today.

Writing Activities:

1. Imagine that you are Dicey. Write a journal entry for the day you chased Ellen from the pump. Record your thoughts and feelings about Ellen, and tell why you bully her.

2. Write about a time when you were threatened by a bully. Describe the event and tell how you reacted. As you look back upon the time, do you wish you had acted in a different way?

CHAPTERS 3, 4

Vocabulary: Draw a line from each word or phrase on the left to its definition on the right. Then use the numbered words to fill in the blanks in the sentences below.

1. disheveled
2. ailment
3. addled
4. courier
5. breeches
6. unseemly
7. urchin
8. gallows tree

a. messenger sent in haste
b. illness
c. improper
d. rumpled; not neat
e. confused
f. wooden structure consisting of a crossbar on two upright posts, used for hanging criminals
g. trousers
h. poor, ragged child

. . . .

1. The convicted murderer was hanged on a(n) _____.

2. Laughter is _____ at a funeral.

3. The man looked quite _____ after sleeping in his clothes all night.

4. Charles Dickens wrote about a street _____ named Oliver Twist, a poor orphan who became involved with a gang of young pickpockets.

5. After his long illness, my grandfather's brains were so _____ that he didn't even know my name.

6. The doctor diagnosed her _____ as a bad cold.

7. The _____ has an important message for the general.

8. The boy pulled up his _____ before putting on his socks and shoes.

> Read to find out if Ellen has the courage to take on a difficult task.

Questions:

1. How does Ellen feel about the leeches? What does the fact that she intends to use them to treat her grandfather's ankle suggest about her?

2. Why does Grandfather think it is easy for a barber to be a spy?

Chapters 3, 4 (cont.) pp. 32-54

3. How do Ellen and her mother react when Grandfather first suggests that Ellen take the message?

4. What former three acts of courage does Grandfather point out to Ellen when she says that she doesn't have courage?

5. Why is it so important that the bread be delivered? Why can't it be delivered directly to George Washington?

6. How will Ellen get to Elizabeth-town? What will she do once she gets there?

7. Why does Ellen decide to deliver the bread?

8. How does Ellen act once she makes the decision to go? What does this suggest about her?

9. How might Ellen's failure to deliver the bread put Grandfather at risk?

Questions for Discussion:

1. Do you think that Grandfather is right to ask Ellen to deliver the message?

2. Ellen's grandfather says that we get over fear by doing things we think we cannot do. Do you agree with him?

3. Why do you think that it is necessary for Ellen to dress up as a boy to accomplish her mission?

Literary Element: Plot

The plot of a novel is the sequence of events that happen in the story. Conflicts, the struggles between opposing forces, create the story's dramatic tension, moving the plot forward. Describe the following conflicts in this novel:

• Ellen's personal conflict

_____

• Ellen's conflict with another character

_____

• Political conflict

_____

Chapters 3, 4 (cont.)

Social Studies Connection:

Grandfather is afraid that he might hang if he is caught. Do some research to find out about the legal system in colonial America. Where would Grandfather have been tried? Would the judge have been British or American? What kinds of citizens would have made up the jury? For what crimes were people hanged in colonial America?

Writing Activity:

Write about one of your fears. Using descriptive words, tell what you are afraid of and what steps you might take to overcome this fear.

CHAPTERS 5, 6

Vocabulary: Use a word from the Word Box to replace the underlined word or phrase in each of the following sentences. Write the word you choose on the line below the sentence.

> *WORD BOX*
>
> defying   impudent   scraggly   woebegone
> hesitation   jowls   sloops

1. After hiding his sister's homework, the boy had a <u>shamelessly bold</u> grin on his face.

   _____

2. Without a moment's <u>delay</u>, we jumped aboard the train as it pulled away from the station.

   _____

3. We loved to watch the <u>sailboats</u> glide by in the bay.

   _____

4. After a week in the field, a soldier needed the services of a barber to shave his <u>sparse, uneven</u> beard.

   _____

5. It made me sad to see your <u>sorrowful</u> expression when you learned that your brother was too sick to come home for the holidays.

   _____

6. The guard was so angry when I walked into the building that his <u>fleshy, hanging part under his lower jaw</u> shook with rage.

   _____

7. It amused the soldiers to see a small boy <u>boldly resisting</u> them.

   _____

> Read to find out how Ellen faces her first challenges.

Questions:

1. What surprises Ellen about Dicey's behavior when the Brinkerhoff boys gang up against her? What does this suggest about Dicey?

2. What does Ellen do when the Brinkerhoff boys steal her bread? Why is Ellen surprised by her own behavior?

Chapters 5, 6 (cont.) pp. 55-79

3. Why can't the Brinkerhoff boys "catch a girl who held her grandfather's secret snuffbox in her arms"? How does Ellen feel about saving her grandfather's message?

4. What disappointment does Ellen encounter when she finally arrives at the docks?

5. How does Ellen arrive on board a British boat?

6. How does Ellen save her bread from Dow?

Questions for Discussion:

1. What evidence showed that food was scarce in New York in1776? Why do you think food might be scarce during wartime?

2. How is Ellen's character changing as she tries to accomplish her task?

Literary Devices:

I. *Simile*—A simile is a figure of speech in which two unlike objects are compared using the words "like" or "as." For example:

> The men sat on planks and were crowded together as closely as kernels of corn on a cob.

What is being compared?

_____

How does this comparison help you get a clear picture of the scene?

_____

_____

II. *Personification*—Personification is a literary device in which an author grants human qualities to nonhuman objects, animals, or ideas. For example:

> She [Ellen] looked up at the hazy sun that struggled wanly in a gray sky.

What is being personified?

_____

What does this reveal about the weather?

_____

_____

Chapters 5, 6 (cont.)

Social Studies Connection:

Ellen refers to "the great fire" that occurred in September 1776 in New York City. Do some research to find out more about this fire. When did it start? What damage did it cause? Who was suspected of starting the fire?

Writing Activity:

In these chapters Ellen has to do some quick thinking to save her bread. Describe a time when you had to think quickly to solve an immediate problem. How successful was your solution? What, if anything, would you do differently if you faced the same problem again?

CHAPTERS 7, 8

Vocabulary: Synonyms are words with similar meanings. Draw a line from each word in column A to its synonym in column B. Then use the words in column A to fill in the blanks in the sentences below.

<u>A</u>

1. scoffed
2. burly
3. spires
4. ruddy
5. induce
6. bewilderment
7. scrawny
8. amiss

<u>B</u>

a. convince
b. steeples
c. sturdy
d. wrong
e. lean
f. sneered
g. reddish
h. confusion

. . . .

1. Nothing could _____ the mother to leave the bedside of her sick child.

2. People with _____ complexions look healthier than those who are pale.

3. At one time people _____ at the idea of a machine that could be made to fly.

4. After not being fed for a week, the dog appeared _____ and tired.

5. The _____ fighter looked as if he could beat any opponent.

6. I knew something was _____ when I noticed that the door had been forced open.

7. The cathedral had two tall _____.

8. You can imagine my _____ after receiving news that I won a contest I had never entered.

> Read to find out about new challenges Ellen faces when she gets off the boat.

Questions:

1. Why does Dow think that the war will end quickly?

2. How does Ellen respond when Dow calls the colonial soldiers cowards? Why does she respond this way?

Chapters 7, 8 (cont.) pp 80-106

3. How does Higgins respond when Ellen asks if he is ever afraid? What advice does he give her about dealing with fear?

4. How have Ellen's feelings about her mission changed?

5. What problem does Ellen face when she goes ashore?

6. Why does Ellen fear the Hessian soldiers she sees in Perth Amboy?

7. Why is Ellen afraid to walk to Elizabeth-town?

8. Why is Ellen happy to see Higgins? How does Higgins motivate her to walk to Elizabeth-town?

Questions for Discussion:

1. Do you agree with Dow's advice to Ellen about the best way to deal with a bully?

2. Do you think it is possible to face danger, such as an impending battle, without fear?

3. Do you think it is wise for Higgins to encourage Ellen to attempt to walk from Perth Amboy to Elizabeth-town?

Social Studies Connection:

Dow ridicules the clothes worn by the American army. Find illustrations showing the clothing worn by the American soldiers during the Revolutionary War. Then find illustrations of the uniforms worn by the regular British soldiers, the Highlanders, and the Hessians. Which of these uniforms would you have preferred to wear if you were fighting in America in the winter of 1776? Why?

Literary Devices:

I. *Irony*—Irony is a twist of words or events that turns out to be the opposite of what is expected. Why is it ironic that Higgins encouraged Ellen to walk to Elizabeth-town?

_____

_____

_____

_____

Chapters 7, 8 (cont.)

II. *Simile*—What is compared in the following simile:

> With sails set wide, like the wings of a bird, the boat was skimming now instead of straining through the waves.

_____

How does this simile help you visualize the scene?

_____

_____

Literary Element: Characterization

Characters in literature are revealed by what they say and do and by what other people say about them. On each line of the spider maps below write a word or phrase that tells about Ellen and Higgins. Compare your responses with those of your classmates.

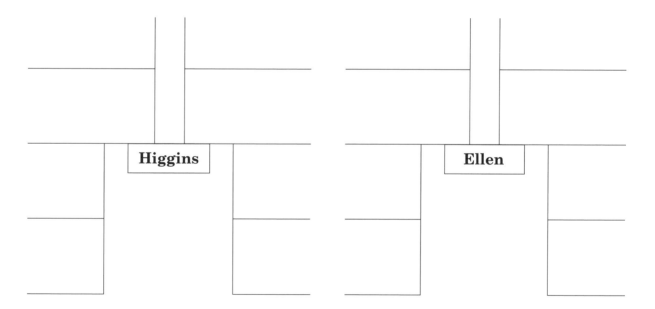

Higgins　　　　　**Ellen**

Writing Activities:

1. Use the words you wrote above to help you write a character sketch of Higgins or Ellen.

2. Imagine you are Higgins. Write a letter to your son in England in which you tell him about your meeting with Ellen Toliver.

CHAPTERS 9, 10

Vocabulary: Analogies are equations in which the first pair of words has the same relationship as the second pair of words. For example, WEALTHY is to POOR as STRONG is to WEAK. Both pairs of words are opposites. Choose the best word from the Word Box to complete each of the analogies below.

WORD BOX			
desperation	hacked	lanky	serene
flecked	hubbub	refugees	

1. FESTIVAL is to CELEBRATION as UPROAR is to _____.

2. JOYOUS is to SAD as _____ is to ANXIOUS.

3. DRENCHED is to SOAKED as SPECKLED is to _____.

4. CONTESTANTS is to COMPETE as _____ is to FLEE.

5. TIRED is to ENERGETIC as STOCKY is to _____.

6. CUT is to _____ as STROLLED is to WALKED.

7. ADMIRATION is to RESPECT as _____ is to HOPELESSNESS.

> Read to find out why Ellen must stand up to a pig.

Questions:

1. As Ellen is walking to Elizabeth-town, what difference does she notice between this walk and the one she took with her mother from Long Island to New York? What explanation does Murdock give for the way people behave in New Jersey?

2. What motivates Ellen to continue on even though she is afraid of traveling through the woods?

3. Why is the route to Elizabeth-town three miles more than Ellen had expected?

4. Why does Murdock offer Ellen a ride? Why does she accept?

5. How does Ellen find out that Murdock is not a Tory?

6. How do Ellen's actions after dropping the bread arouse Murdock's suspicions?

7. Why doesn't Mrs. Murdock want her husband to take Ellen to Elizabeth-town?

Chapters 9, 10 (cont.) p. 107-134

8. Why does Ellen flee from the Murdock's house leaving the bread behind?

9. Why does Ellen have to challenge a hungry pig?

Questions for Discussion:

1. Why do you think a war, such as the American Revolution, caused many people to be refugees?

2. Do you think Mr. Murdock realizes that Ellen is on a spying mission?

3. What are the many ways that the once-timid Ellen is now displaying courage?

Literary Devices:

I. *Building Suspense*—High interest in the outcome of a story is called suspense. The author builds suspense by putting the welfare of a character in danger, and leaving the reader uncertain of the outcome. In what ways does the author build suspense in these chapters of *Toliver's Secret*?

    _____

    _____

    _____

    _____

    _____

II. *Simile*—What is being compared in the following simile?

    . . . she tucked it [the loaf of bread] up under her jacket where it
    sat like a lump of ice on her stomach.

    _____

    What is the effect of this comparison?

    _____

    _____

Chapters 9, 10 (cont.)

Social Studies Connection:

Find all the words to "The Liberty Tree." Then locate and read some more of Thomas Paine's writings. What do they all have in common? Why did he write them? What effect did they have on the events of his time?

Writing Activities:

1. Mr. Murdock is vehemently opposed to the British, but Mrs. Murdock approves of King George. Imagine that you are one of these characters. Write a short essay defending your viewpoint. Be sure to give specific reasons.

2. Write about a time when your fears turned out to be groundless. Tell whether this experience helped you deal with future fears.

CHAPTERS 11 – 13

Vocabulary: Use the context to determine the meaning of the underlined word in each of the following sentences. Then compare your definition with a dictionary definition.

1. The soldiers in the tavern drank ale out of <u>tankards</u>.

   Your definition _____

   Dictionary definition _____

2. In countries where sheep are plentiful, roast <u>mutton</u> is often a popular dish.

   Your definition _____

   Dictionary definition _____

3. The actress made a <u>curtsy</u> when the audience gave her a standing ovation.

   Your definition _____

   Dictionary definition _____

4. The sailor moved the <u>tiller</u> to steer the boat away from the rocks.

   Your definition _____

   Dictionary definition _____

5. Standing on the bank of the river, we watched the <u>scow</u> hauling garbage from the city.

   Your definition _____

   Dictionary definition _____

6. Once he had taken karate lessons, he was no longer afraid of the <u>rowdy</u> boys in the street.

   Your definition _____

   Dictionary definition _____

7. General Washington took time to <u>fortify</u> his winter headquarters so that the British could not easily attack.

   Your definition _____

   Dictionary definition _____

> Read to find out if Ellen accomplishes her task.

Chapters 11 – 13 (cont.) pp. 135 -166

Questions:

1. How does Ellen overcome her fears of the dark woods to continue on her journey?

2. Why do the blacksmith and the other man at the blacksmith shop make Ellen nervous? Why is the man interested in Ellen?

3. What bad news awaits Ellen at the tavern? How does she react to this news?

4. What evidence shows that Mistress Shannon is risking her life for the Patriots' cause?

5. What convinces Ellen that the man she met at the blacksmith shop is really Mr. Shannon?

6. What information will Ellen be able to give her grandfather as a result of her detour to Perth Amboy?

7. When Ellen returns to New York, how is her reaction to her surroundings different from what it was before? How does her changed attitude affect the way she deals with Dicey?

8. What mixed emotions do Ellen's mother and grandfather feel about Ellen's experiences?

9. Why was Washington able to surprise and defeat the British at Trenton?

10. What good news does the family receive? Why does someone send Ellen a silver locket?

Questions for Discussion:

1. Were there any clues to suggest that the big man was Mr. Shannon? Was there any way that Ellen could have discovered the man's identity, or was she right to flee?

2. Why do you think spying was very important to the Patriots' cause?

3. Why do you think Ellen pretends that the locket is from General Washington? Who might be the sender? Why do you think the person remained anonymous?

Literary Devices:

I. *Personification*—What is being personified in the following example?

> It seemed to her that their [the trees'] branches were arms—
> moving, groaning, bending low to grab her.

_____

How does this language help express Ellen's feelings as she makes her way through the dark woods?

_____

_____

Chapters 11 – 13 (cont.)

II. *Onomatopoeia*—Onomatopoeia is the use of a word that imitates or suggests the sound of the object it describes. Some examples of onomatopoeia are the words "snap," "buzz," and "hum." Write the examples of onomatopoeia in the following sentences adapted from the novel:

- A dog barked at the sound of her crunching in the snow.

_____

- Ellen knew it was the doorway of a blacksmith's shop by the clang of a hammer on an iron anvil.

_____

- On a spit before the fire a roast of mutton was sizzling and sputtering.

_____

Why do you think the author used this device?

_____

_____

_____

Science Connection:

Review the events in *Toliver's Secret* and consider which of the problems Ellen faced would have been eliminated if today's means of communication and transportation were available to her.

Writing Activities:

1. Imagine you are Ellen. Write a letter to Ezra telling him about your adventure and how you think it has changed you.

2. By now you probably have some idea of what was in the message Ellen's grandfather put in the snuffbox. Use your imagination and information from the novel to write that message.

Chapters 11 – 13 (cont.)

Literary Element: Character Development

Use the Venn diagram below to compare Ellen's character at the beginning of the novel to Ellen's character at the end of the novel. Use the overlapping portion of the circles to record those aspects of Ellen's personality that have remained the same.

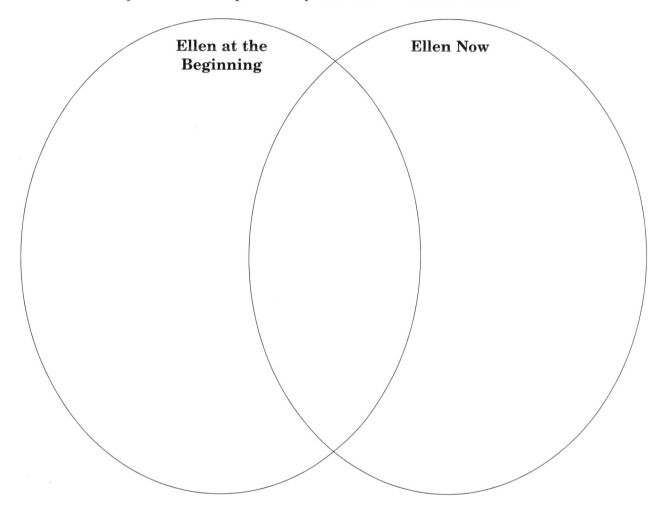

CLOZE ACTIVITY

The following passage has been taken from Chapter Eleven of the novel. Read it through completely and then go back and fill in each blank with a word that makes sense. Afterwards you may compare your language with that of the author.

On either side of the road the trees stood black against the dark sky. It seemed to her that their branches were _____[1]—moving, groaning, bending low to grab her. _____[2] tried to remember the friendly look of _____[3] trees in the late afternoon light. But _____[4] were more frightening. Each hair seemed to _____[5] up straight on her head, and she _____[6] on her cap to hold them down.

"_____[7] only the trees and they can't hurt _____,"[8] she said over and over. "And that _____[9] sound—it's only the wind." With sharp _____,[10] it whipped angrily around her cold wet _____.[11]

Ellen was all alone but she was _____[12] with a stubborn will. Nothing was going _____[13] stop her now that she was only _____[14] a mile from Mr. Shannon's tavern.

Whenever she _____[15] a dark shadow of a farmhouse sitting _____[16] of a stone wall, she could smell the _____[17] from the chimney. They must be people _____.[18] People eating bowls of piping hot stew, _____[19] beside a crackling fire. Perhaps children were _____[20] on nightshirts that had been warmed at _____[21] fire. Perhaps they were climbing into bed _____[22] putting their feet against warm bricks wrapped _____[23] wool. Mother had always warmed her bed _____[24] her this way at home.

Not a _____[25] of light showed at the windows. Although _____[26] dog barked at the sound of her _____[27] crunching in the snow, the doors remained _____.[28]

And then, far ahead, she saw a light no bigger than a needle prick in the dark.

POST-READING ACTIVITIES

1. Return to the K-W-L chart on the American Revolution that you began on page five of this study guide. Fill in column three and compare your responses with those of your classmates.

2. Imagine you are a journalist during the time of the American Revolution. Write an article in which you report on one of the battles mentioned in the novel. Do some additional research to get the necessary background information for your article.

3. **Art Activity:** Create a shoe box diorama showing a scene of your choice from the novel. You might wish to find illustrations in books about colonial life to help you.

4. **Cooperative Learning Activity:** A theme is a central idea or message that is carried throughout the book. Work in a cooperative learning group with classmates who have read *Toliver's Secret* to trace the following themes as they appear throughout the story:
   - courage
   - maturity and responsibility
   - patriotism
   - belief in oneself

5. The events in *Toliver's Secret* take place in December 1776. The Revolutionary War did not end until 1763. Write a short sequel to the novel that takes place in 1783. In your sequel tell what life is like for Ellen and her family after the war.

6. With a small group of classmates, role-play any of the following hypothetical scenes:
   - After Ellen leaves on her mission, Ellen's mother and grandfather discuss their hopes for the future.
   - Higgins and Dow discuss their encounter with Toliver.
   - Dicey tells the Brinkerhoff boys how Ellen has changed.
   - After Ezra returns home, he and Ellen discuss their adventures during the war.

7. The novel mentions many different kinds of colonial occupations—barber, schoolmaster, candlemaker, soldier, carpenter, drayman, cobbler, tavern owner, oysterman, farmer, and blacksmith. Choose one of these or another colonial occupation to research. Pretend that you practiced this occupation in 1776. Present an oral report to the class in which you describe your typical workday.

8. There are many songs mentioned in this novel. Make a list of these and then do research to find the words to as many of them as possible. With your classmates, create a songbook of the popular British and Yankee songs of 1776.

Post-Reading Activities (cont.)

9. Ellen saves her loaf of bread by giving Dow the corncakes in her pocket. Cornbread and corncakes were staples of the colonial diet. The bread and cakes differed in shape, but the basic ingredients were always the same—cornmeal, salt, and water. Make corncakes for your family. Here is a recipe to try.

Corncakes

What you need:

1 cup yellow cornmeal   1 cup boiling water
1 teaspoon salt   1 cup milk

What you do:

1. In a bowl mix together the cornmeal and salt.

2. Add the boiling water, stirring until smooth.

3. Add the milk. Stir well.

4. Grease a heavy, 12-inch frying pan. Set over medium-low heat.

5. Drop tablespoonsful of the batter onto the pan. Cook until golden, about 5 minutes. Turn the cakes carefully with a spatula. Cook the other side 5 minutes.

6. Serve hot or cold, with butter and maple syrup. This recipe makes 12-15 cakes.

---

10. Work with a partner to create a board game based on *Toliver's Secret*. The object for each player might be to move across the board from New York to Perth Amboy and to Elizabeth-town as a final destination. Impediments along the way might be the Hudson River, British soldiers, a forest, etc. These could be represented as penalty boxes.

11. **Literature Circle:** Have a literature circle discussion in which you tell your personal reactions to *Toliver's Secret*. Here are some questions and sentence starters to help your circle begin a discussion.
    * How are you like Ellen? How are you different?
    * Do you find the characters in the novel realistic? Why or why not?
    * Which character did you like the most? The least?
    * What were the most interesting things you learned about the historical period in which the book was set?
    * Who else would you like to read this novel? Why?
    * What questions would you like to ask the author about this novel?
    * It was not fair when . . .
    * I would have liked to see . . .
    * I wonder . . .
    * Ellen learned that . . .

SUGGESTIONS FOR FURTHER READING

* Avi, *The Fighting Ground*. HarperCollins.

*#Collier, James L., and Christopher Collier. *My Brother Sam is Dead*. Scholastic.

* _____. *War Comes to Willy Freeman*. Random House.

* Dalgliesch, Alice. *The Courage of Sarah Noble*. Simon & Schuster.

   Edmondo, Walter D. *The Matchlock Gun*. Penguin.

*#Fast, Howard. *April Morning*. Random House.

*#Forbes, Esther. *Johnny Tremain*. Random House.

* Fritz, Jean. *The Cabin Faced West*. Penguin.

   _____. *Early Thunder*. Penguin.

   Gauch, Patricia L. *Aaron and the Green Mountain Boys*. Shoe Tree.

* Hunt, Irene. *Across Five Aprils*. Berkley.

* Lawson, Robert. *Ben and Me*. Little, Brown.

* McGovern, Ann. *The Secret Soldier*. Scholastic.

* O'Dell, Scott. *Sarah Bishop*. Random House.

*#Speare, Elizabeth. *The Witch of Blackbird Pond*. Random House.

   Taylor, David. *Farewell to Valley Forge*. HarperCollins.

* Woodruff, Elvira. *George Washington's Socks*. Scholastic.

   Yerby, Frank. *Bride of Liberty*. Pyramid.

Some Other Books by Esther Wood Brady

Belinda Blue. Longmans, Green.

Ezra, Nehemiah, and Esther. Abingdon Press.

Great Sweeping Days. Longmans, Green.

The House in the Hoo. Longmans, Green.

Pedro's Coconut Skates. Longmans, Green.

Pepper Moon. Longmans, Green.

Silk and Satin Lane. Longmans, Green.

Silver Widgeon. Longmans, Green.

The Toad on Capitol Hill. Random House.

Wish on Capitol Hill. Random House.

* NOVEL-TIES study guides are available for these titles.

\# HISTORICAL-TIES Study Guide entitled *Colonial American and the Revolution* includes these titles.

ANSWER KEY

Pre-Reading Activities

  (3) Pro-American—Patriots, General Washington, Rebels, Thomas Paine, Yankees; Pro-British—General Cornwallis, General Howe, Tories, King George III, Lobsterbacks, Hessians, Redcoats; (5) 1. b 2. f 3. a 4. d 5. e 6. c

Chapters 1, 2

Vocabulary: Across—1. pendulum 3. impish 6. waistcoat 9. blustering 10. tavern 14. nimbly 15. smirking 16. roister; Down—2. mimic 4. haughtily 5. drayman 7. snuffbox 8. jauntily 11. rafters 12. auburn 13. minuet

Questions: 1. Ellen thinks that her grandfather has lost his wits when she sees him slipping into the dark kitchen and locking the door, then pinning the window curtains together with a knitting needle. His behavior suggests that he is doing something that could get him into trouble. 2. Ellen's grandfather presses his snuffbox into bread dough. He gruffly and adamantly warns her not to speak of what she has seen. 3. British soldiers are living in Grandfather's house because the colonists were responsible for quartering British soldiers after New York fell to the British three months earlier. 4. It is clear that Grandfather and his family do not support the British because they resent quartering British soldiers and ridicule them behind their backs. Ellen and her mother are unhappy that they must dress the soldier's wigs. 5. Ellen does not like to go to the pump because she is afraid of a bully named Dicey. Ellen's grandfather thinks Ellen should stand up to Dicey, while her mother feels she should just go to another pump. 6. Ellen's father and brother went to fight in the Battle of Brooklyn Heights; her father was killed, and her brother's whereabouts are unknown. Ellen and her mother were left to fend for themselves, and eventually had to walk ten miles to New York to stay with Ellen's grandfather. 7. A barber during colonial times would perform quasi-medical functions—particularly the practices of bleeding and leeching. 8. Dicey is a rough bully who picks on those smaller than she. Ellen is timid and easily intimidated by the bold girl. 9. While Ellen is out getting water, Grandfather falls on the ice and sprains his ankle.

Chapters 3, 4

Vocabulary: 1. d 2. b 3. e 4. a 5. g 6. c 7. h 8. f; 1. gallows tree 2. unseemly 3. disheveled 4. urchin 5. addled 6. ailment 7. courier 8. breeches

Questions: 1. Ellen finds the leeches horrible and fears them but she will use them on her grandfather. This suggests that Ellen has the courage to overcome her fears. 2. Grandfather thinks it is easy for a barber to be a spy and get behind enemy lines because the men will always need a shave and his leeches. 3. Both Ellen and her mother think that Ellen is too young and timid to take the message and the task is too risky. 4. Grandfather recalls that Ellen walked ten miles to New York with her mother; she and her mother stayed all alone in their house with war all around them; and Ellen brought the leeches to put on Grandfather's ankle. 5. There is a message for General Washington in the bread. The information about the British might help Washington reverse the three months of defeat his army has suffered. It is too risky to deliver the bread with the message inside directly to George Washington. There is less risk that it be intercepted if there are a series of couriers. 6. Ellen is to sail to Elizabeth-town on a farmer's or oysterman's boat. Once there, she is to give the bread to Mr. Shannon at the Jolly Fox Tavern. 7. Ellen decides to deliver the bread because she realizes that her grandfather wouldn't put her in danger, she is convinced that the message is important, and she begins to believe that she might be up to the task after all. 8. Once she makes the decision to go, Ellen eagerly tries on Ezra's clothes and confidently instructs her mother to cut her hair short. This suggests that she is conquering her fear and gaining confidence that she can deliver the bread. 9. Grandfather might hang if the message is intercepted by British soldiers or Loyalists.

Chapters 5, 6

Vocabulary: 1. impudent 2. hesitation 3. sloops 4. scraggly 5. woebegone 6. jowls 7. defying

Questions: 1. Ellen is surprised that Dicey cries and runs away when the Brinkerhoff boys gang up against her. This suggests that Dicey is not as bold as Ellen imagines. 2. When the Brinkerhoff boys steal

her bread, Ellen shouts in a loud, strong voice, runs after the boys, and hits one of them with a broom handle. Ellen surprises herself because she is acting in a bolder manner than she had ever done before. 3. Ellen, entrusted with her grandfather's secret, finds the strength to outrun the boys because she is determined to keep it safe. She feels proud of herself and more confident. 4. When Ellen arrives at the docks, she finds that the oystermen's and farmers' boats have already sailed, and only boats filled with British soldiers remain. 5. Ellen arrives on board a British ship when a hungry soldier who wants to eat Ellen's bread whisks her aboard. 6. Ellen snatches the bread back from Dow, tucks it under her jacket, doubles up, and locks her arms beneath her legs.

Chapters 7, 8

Vocabulary: 1. f 2. c 3. b 4. g 5. a 6. h 7. e 8. d; 1. induce 2. ruddy 3. scoffed 4. scrawny 5. burly 6. amiss 7. spires 8. bewilderment

Questions: 1. Dow thinks the war will end quickly because the colonial soldiers are outnumbered and under-trained. Also, he uses the recent defeats of the colonial soldiers at Fort Washington and Fort Lee as points of reference. 2. When Dow calls the colonial soldiers cowards, Ellen strongly protests. She responds this way because her feeling of patriotism outweighs her fear of Dow. 3. Higgins admits to being afraid at times, but adds that this is nothing to be ashamed of. He advises Ellen that if something is important to her she must conquer her fear and do the task. 4. At first the mission was important to Ellen because of its importance to her grandfather; now she is eager to accomplish the mission to help General Washington. 5. When Ellen goes ashore, she realizes that the boat is docked in Perth Amboy, not Elizabeth-town. 6. Ellen fears the Hessian soldiers because she knows that they are hired soldiers who are reputed to be particularly fierce on the battlefield. 7. Ellen fears walking to Elizabeth-town because she is in an unfamiliar area and has never walked ten miles alone before. 8. Ellen is happy to see Higgins because she views him as her only friend in strange surroundings. Ellen is motivated to walk ten miles at night in a strange place by Higgins's confidence in her ability and his friendship.

Chapters 9, 10

Vocabulary: 1. hubbub 2. serene 3. flecked 4. refugees 5. lanky 6. hacked 7. desperation

Questions: 1. Ellen notices on her walk that the people in New Jersey keep to themselves, while those in New York had been friendly to her and her mother. Murdock explains that the people in New Jersey fear the British soldiers. 2. Ellen is motivated by Higgins's advice about facing a difficult task: "Just square your shoulders and start." 3. Ellen had been told that the distance between Perth Amboy and Elizabeth-town was ten miles. The twisting road through the forest adds three extra miles. 4. Murdock offers Ellen a ride because he needs someone to hold his baskets, or he might just want to help the child. Ellen accepts because she doesn't think she can walk the additional miles to Elizabeth-town. 5. It is clear that Murdock is not a Tory because he talks angrily about the British soldiers and King George. 6. When Ellen drops the bread, she jumps off the horse and retrieves it from a stream without thinking about the danger, causing Murdock to wonder why anyone would go through all that trouble just for a loaf of bread. 7. Mrs. Murdock does not want her husband to take Ellen to Elizabeth-town because she is afraid he will be shot, leaving her a widow with four boys to raise. 8. Mrs. Murdock wants to remove Ellen's wet breeches, and Ellen fears the woman will discover that she is a girl. In her haste to escape Mrs. Murdock, Ellen forgets that the bread is drying by the fire. 9. When Mrs. Murdock throws the precious bread she had left behind to a pig, Ellen grabs the bread from the animal.

Chapters 11 – 13

Vocabulary: 1. tankards–large drinking mugs 2. mutton–flesh of a sheep used as food 3. curtsy–bow of respect or greeting by females, made by bending the knees and lowering the body slightly 4. tiller–bar at the stern used to turn the rudder in steering a boat 5. scow–flat-bottomed boat used to carry freight 6. rowdy–rough, disorderly, quarrelsome 7. fortify–strengthen against attack

Questions: 1. To overcome her fears, Ellen thinks about how she bravely fought the pig, talks to herself to calm down, and stubbornly sets her mind to the task at hand. 2. The blacksmith and the other man make Ellen nervous when they question her about the objects she is hiding under her jacket. The big man is Mr. Shannon and suspects that Ellen might have something to do with the message he expects. 3. Ellen is distressed to learn that Mr. Shannon has gone away and will not

return for several days. She will not give the bread to anyone but Mr. Shannon as she was instructed. 4. Mistress Shannon is so worried that her Patriot sympathies will be discovered by the British soldiers who come to her tavern that she wears a British flag in her hair and is very friendly to the British soldiers whom she hates. She is so worried about the risks that she and her husband are taking that she does not trust Ellen, who appears to be a little waif when she comes to the tavern. 5. Ellen realizes that the man she met at the blacksmith shop is really Mr. Shannon when he reveals that he knows about her grandfather and the bread that is supposed to be a birthday present for him. 6. As a result of her detour to Perth Amboy, Ellen will be able to give her grandfather details about the British mobilization that she witnessed. 7. When Ellen returns to New York, she is no longer a fearful, timid child. Now, she stands up to Dicey, and the bully backs down. 8. When Ellen's mother and grandfather hear Ellen recount her experiences delivering the message in the bread, they have mixed emotions of pride in her accomplishments and guilt for subjecting such a young girl to serious danger. 9. George Washington and his troops were able to surprise and defeat the British at Trenton because he had gotten so much good information about British troop activity from citizens such as Ellen. 10. The family receives the good news that General Washington took the city of Trenton and had another victory at Princeton; and that Ezra is safe in Morristown. Ellen receives the locket as thanks for her part in helping General Washington.